EYES

Shannon Caster

Rosen Classroom

For my parents, T. J. and Sara

Published in 2010 by The Rosen Publishing Group, Inc.
29 East 21st Street, New York, NY 10010

First Edition

Editor: Joanne Randolph
Book Design: Greg Tucker
Layout Design: Kate Laczynski
Photo Researcher: Jessica Gerweck

Photo Credits: Cover © www.istockphoto.com/Kateryna Govorushchenko; cover (inset), pp. 5, 13 (inset) Nucleus Medical Art, Inc./Getty Images; p. 6 Bernhard Lang/Getty Images; pp. 6 (inset), 17 (inset) © www.istockphoto.com/Nurbek Sagynbaev; pp. 9, 10 (inset), 14 (inset) 3D4Medical.com/Getty Images; p. 10 Peter Essick/Getty Images; p. 13 Peter Dazeley/Getty Images; p. 14 Shutterstock.com; p. 17 www.istockphoto.com/Judy Barranco; p. 18 Justin Pumfrey/Getty Images; p. 18 (inset) 3DClinic/Getty Images; 21 Symphonie/Getty Images; p. 21 (inset) DEA Picture Library/Getty Images.

Library of Congress Cataloging-in-Publication Data

Caster, Shannon.
    Eyes / Shannon Caster. — 1st ed.
        p. cm. — (Body works)
    Includes index.
    ISBN 978-1-4358-9369-6 (library binding) — ISBN 978-1-4358-9826-4 (pbk.) —
ISBN 978-1-4358-9827-1 (6-pack)
    1. Eye—Juvenile literature. 2. Vision—Juvenile literature. I. Title.
    QP475.7.C36 2010
    612.8'4—dc22

                                                                      2009034086

Manufactured in the United States of America

CPSIA Compliance Information: Batch #WW10PK: For Further Information contact Rosen Publishing, New York, New York at 1-800-237-9932

Contents

Eyes on the World

Your eyes are your windows to the world. Every day, they take in information, or facts, about light, color, shape, movement, and the distance of things around you. Then the eyes send this information to the brain. As part of the body's **sensory system**, the eyes work with the brain to give you your sense of sight.

The eye is an **organ** made up of three main layers. The outer layer consists of the cornea and sclera. The iris, lens, and ciliary muscle make up the middle layer. Finally, the retina and optic nerve make up the inner layer of the eye.

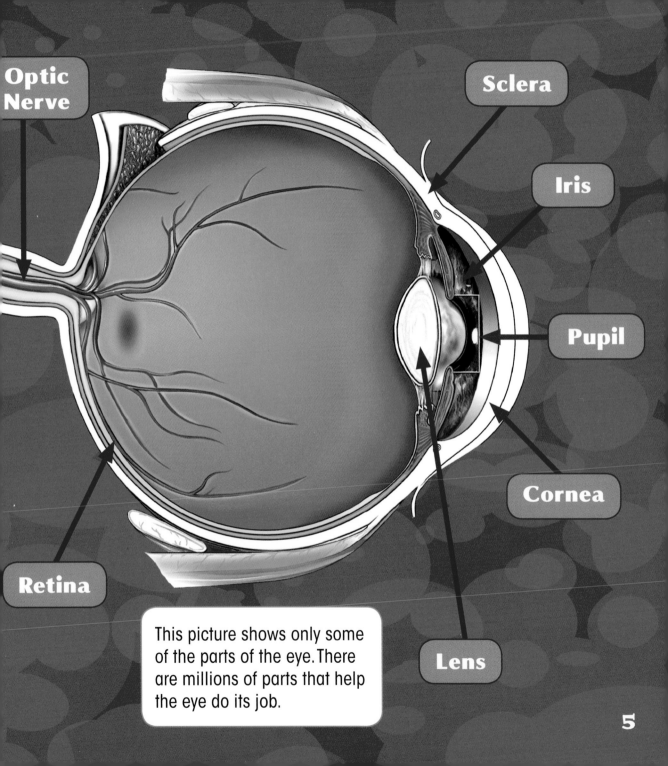

Optic Nerve

Sclera

Iris

Pupil

Cornea

Retina

Lens

This picture shows only some of the parts of the eye. There are millions of parts that help the eye do its job.

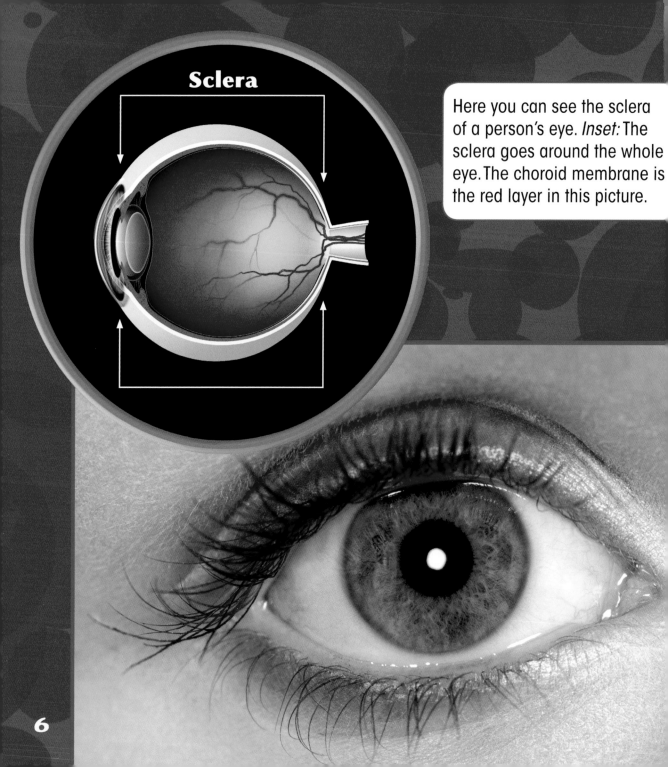

Sclera

Here you can see the sclera of a person's eye. *Inset:* The sclera goes around the whole eye. The choroid membrane is the red layer in this picture.

What Is the Sclera?

When you look into a mirror or at another person, you can easily see the white part of the eye. This firm, white **tissue** is called the sclera. It goes from the front part of your eye to the back. The sclera keeps the inner parts of your eye safe from injury. It also helps give the eye its round shape.

If you look closely at the white part of your eye, you might notice tiny red **blood vessels**. These are actually just below the sclera on the choroid, which is a thin **membrane** between the sclera and the retina. These blood vessels provide important **nutrients** to your eye and carry away waste.

Window to the Eyes

In the very front of your eye is a clear, **transparent** part called the cornea. The cornea acts like a window, letting light pass into your eye. The cornea takes the incoming light rays and bends, or refracts, them onto your lens and retina. It does this to help focus the light at the back of the eye. Most of your eyes' focusing power comes from your cornea.

Your cornea does not have blood vessels in it. Instead, the cornea gets nutrients from a liquid in the eye called the **aqueous humor**. This liquid is found in a part of the eye called the anterior chamber, which is right behind the cornea.

Anterior Chamber

Cornea

Here you can see the cornea and the anterior chamber. The aqueous humor is pumped through the pupil to the anterior chamber from a chamber behind the iris.

There are three kinds of tears made by our tear ducts (inset). Emotional tears are the ones we cry when we are angry or sad.

Tear Duct

Tear Ducts at Work

The cornea counts on tear ducts to stay clean and healthy. When you get a small piece of dirt in your eye, your brain sends messages to your tear ducts to produce a liquid that is like salty water as you blink. This liquid helps wash your eyeball. The tear ducts also produce tears when you cry. Sometimes these tears fill up your eyes and overflow onto your cheeks.

Even when you are not crying or do not have dirt stuck in your eye, the tear ducts give off a small amount of liquid when you blink. This liquid keeps your eye wet and clean.

The Iris and Pupil

Two easily recognizable parts of your eyes are the iris and pupil. The iris is the colored part of the eye. The pupil is the black hole in the middle of the iris.

The main job of the iris is to change the size of the pupil to let the right amount of light into your eye. When it is bright, muscles in the iris **contract**, making the pupil smaller. This lets less light enter the eyes. When it is dark, different muscles in the iris contract to make the pupil dilate, or become larger. This allows more light to enter the eyes so you can see even in dim light.

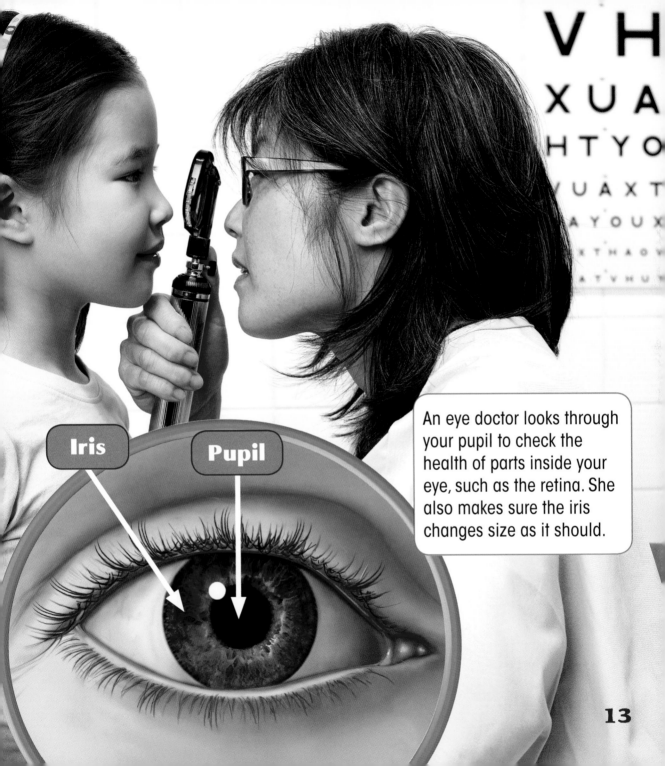

Iris

Pupil

An eye doctor looks through your pupil to check the health of parts inside your eye, such as the retina. She also makes sure the iris changes size as it should.

V H
X U A
H T Y O
V U A X T
A Y O U X

13

Cornea

Scleral Spur

Major Arterial Circle of Iris

Ciliary Muscle

Ciliary Process

A camera lens focuses in much the same way your eye does. *Inset:* The ciliary muscles help change the shape of the lens so you can see clearly.

The Lens and Ciliary Muscles

The lens of your eye works much like a camera lens. When light hits the lens, it is bent so that the light rays **converge** into a clear image. If the images are not clear, the lens changes shape to focus on them better.

At the top and bottom of the lens are the ciliary muscles. When you focus on objects far away, the ciliary muscles pull the lens into a flat, narrow shape. This is because the light does not need to bend as much. To focus on objects close up, the ciliary muscles make the lens fat and round.

Picture This: The Retina ──

Your retina is at the back of your eye. It is made up of millions of cells called rods and cones. It is in the retina that images are changed into **nerve impulses** that can be sent to the brain.

Interestingly enough, the images the retina sends to your brain are actually upside down. This is because as the light enters your cornea and lens, it is bent so it converges into a single point. When the light rays converge, they cross through the single point at an angle and continue on to the retina. By the time the light hits your retina, the image is upside down.

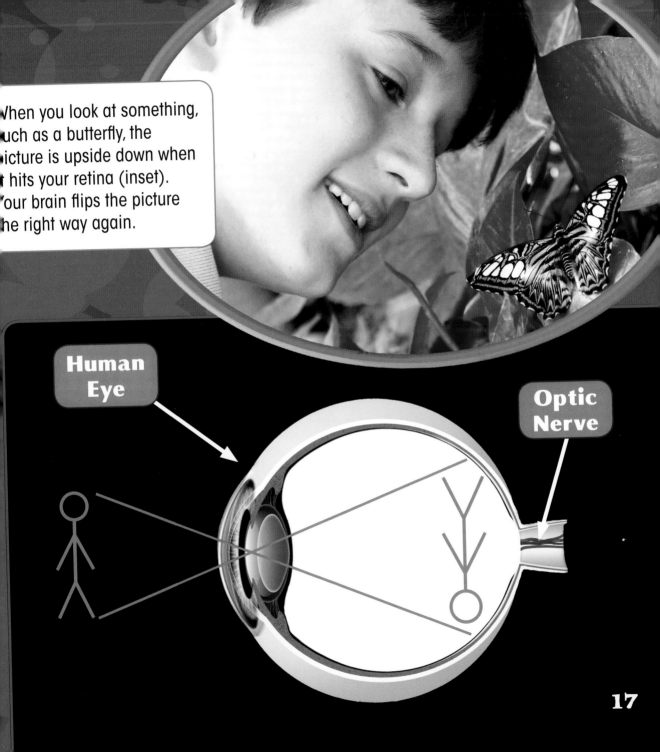

When you look at something, such as a butterfly, the picture is upside down when it hits your retina (inset). Your brain flips the picture the right way again.

Human Eye

Optic Nerve

We can see colors, such as these green plants and the yellow watering can, because of our eyes' cones. *Inset:* Here you can see a rod (left) and a cone (right).

Sense This: The Rods and Cones

The retina's two types of sensory cells are responsible for absorbing, or taking in, light that hits the back of your eye. The rods are long and narrow. They see black and white and work best in dim light. The cones pick up color and work best in brighter light. Rods and cones work as a team so that you can see in many different kinds of light.

Your rods and cones work in almost the same way. When light waves hit the rods and cones, they cause **chemicals** to break down. These chemicals then send electric signals to your brain through the optic nerve.

What a Trip!

After the eyes take a picture of images entering the eye, electric signals are sent to your brain through your optic nerve. The optic nerve is like a pathway that electric signals follow. Each eye has an optic nerve that crisscrosses in your brain. This means images seen in the right eye will travel to the left side of the brain. Images from the left eye will travel to the right side of your brain.

The brain processes, or makes sense of, these signals. Then the brain takes all the information about the color, shape, distance, and movement of objects around you and puts it together as a **three-dimensional** picture.

Optic Nerve

This boy's optic nerves (inset) are sending lots of data to his brain as he quickly moves to catch the soccer ball. There are about 1.1 million nerve cells in each optic nerve.

Eye Trouble

When people have trouble seeing, they are said to have vision problems. A nearsighted person can see things close up, but objects far away are blurry. A farsighted person can clearly see objects far away but not those that are near. When we have trouble seeing clearly, doctors give us glasses or contact lenses to help our eyes focus the light better.

Pink eye is another common eye problem. When the lining of your eye gets infected, it swells up and turns pink. Pink eye can be **contagious**, but careful hand washing can help keep your eyes and body healthy.

Glossary

aqueous humor (AY-kwee-us HYOO-mer) Clear liquid, or watery matter, between the iris and the cornea that give the eye food and helps give the eye its shape.

blood vessels (BLUD VEH-sulz) Narrow tubes in the body through which blood flows.

chemicals (KEH-mih-kulz) Matter that can be mixed with other matter to cause changes.

contagious (kun-TAY-jus) Can be passed on.

contract (kun-TRAKT) To pull together and get shorter.

converge (kun-VERJ) To meet at a point.

membrane (MEM-brayn) A soft, thin layer of living matter.

nerve impulses (NERV IM-puls-ez) Electric signals that cells use to send messages to one another.

nutrients (NOO-tree-unts) Food that a living thing needs to live and grow.

organ (OR-gen) A part inside the body that does a job.

sensory system (SENTS-ree SIS-tem) Organs that give us one of the five senses of sight, touch, taste, smell, and sound.

three-dimensional (three-deh-MENCH-nul) Having height, width, and depth. A flat picture, such as a photo, is two-dimensional. A person is three-dimensional.

tissue (TIH-shoo) Matter that forms the parts of living things.

transparent (tranz-PER-ent) Can be seen through.

Index

Web Sites

Due to the changing nature of Internet links, PowerKids Press has developed an online list of Web sites related to the subject of this book. This site is updated regularly. Please use this link to access the list:
www.powerkidslinks.com/hybw/eyes/